PROPERTY OF:

_____

_____

PSALM 126:2-3

THEN OUR MOUTHS WERE FILLED WITH LAUGHTER

CLEAN BIBLE JOKES

for

Pastors, Family & Co-workers

What are God's favorite music groups?

Genesis & Peter, Paul and Mary.

Who don't Vampires and Jesus like Crypto?

There is staking involved.

What does Rabbis, King Solomon and Abraham Lincoln all have in common?

Temples.

What does Christianity and McDonald's have in common?

Over a billion served and still counting.

What do Will Smith and Goliath the Giant have in common?

Both their careers were hindered by a rock.

What does motion picture science fiction aliens and Jesus have in common?

They both came in peace.

Sally's new little sister was loudly crying non-stop

She asked, "Where did she come from?

The stressed but, polite parents replied, "She is a blessing from heaven."

Sally said, "I see why they did not want her there."

Why was Jesus frugal and cheap?

Jesus saves.

What is The Pope's favorite book in the Bible?

Romans.

Who was the first DJ in the world?

Jesus. He turned tables.

What is Mary's favorite movie?

Silence of the lambs.

What do married men have today. But, Adam did not have?

A nasty mother-in-law.

Why were all the birds on Noah's Ark kept separate from all other animals?

They were fowl.

What do we deal with now, but, Adam and Even did not have to deal with?

Noisy Neighbors

What does Simon Cowell, Thurgood Marshall and Judy Sheindlin all have in common?

Judges is their favorite book in the Bible.

What day did God create laundry?

The day he separated the lights and darks.

Why did Noah and his family run out of food on the arc?

They only had two bucks.

Why would Jesus be a great magician?

He could break any chain.

What does a bad choir, a mother in law and a fine wine have in common?

Too much of them will give you a headache.

One day, three boys were talking over whose Dad was the best at his job.

The first kid said, "My Dad is the best because he is a rich stock broker on Wall Street."

The second kid said, "That's nothing. My Dad is a politician and the most powerful man in the state."

The third kid, a preacher's son said, "Ok. But, my Dad owns Hell."
The other two boys aske how could your dad own hell?

The third kid explained, "When my Dad came home last night and told my mom the the Preacher's Board gave it to him."

What is the bad thing about rumors, gossip and farts?

Sometimes they just come out.

Who is the most sacrilegious and blashemous person in the bible?

Moses, in his anger he broke all ten Commandments at once.

Did you know Jesus is one of the top MMA fighters in the world?

When he is in trouble physically, he just turns the table.

What does church sermons and comedy club comedian jokes have in common?

The audience is waiting for the climax of the story.

Why did Saint Peter allow the lawyer into heaven?

Because, Hell was full.

Jesus fed 2 large masses. It was 5000 one time and 4000 on the other. What food was he determined not to have?

Steak.

A dying lawyer was skimming throught the Bible.

He was looking for loopholes

Recently, a preacher sold his special donkey to a man.The preacher explained, the donkey would go forward on saying"Hallelujah." But, stops when you say "Amen."

The man got on the donkey and yelled "Hallelujah!". The donkey took off. The pair traveled a very long time. They traveled through different towns then through mountains, hills and valleys.

Then the man saw the donkey was head for a cliff, but could not think of the stop word. So he prayed, and finished his prayer with "Amen." Luckily, the donkey stopped one step before the edge of the cliff.
HALLELUJAH, shouted the man.

What's the difference between a lawyer and God?

God does not think he is a lawyer.

But, a lawyer thinks he is God.

Why do people find it difficult to trust doctors, lawyers and pastors?

Because, they are all practicing their professions.

What are David's, King Solomons's and Moses' favorite Television shows?

Big Love and Sister Wives.

Did you know computers and technology is mentioned in the Bible.

God gave Moses two tablets.

A Priest, Rabbi, Imam, Jesus, Moses and the Devil, walk into a bar.

The bartender goes, "Is this a joke?"

What was
William
Shakespeare's
favorite book of
the Bible?

Acts.

What did God say to Adam, Eve, and the serpent after their punishments?

How about those apples?

What is Jesus's least favorite music band?

Judas Priest.

A Preacher sits next to a cowboy on a flight. After the plane takes off, the cowboy asks for a whiskey and soda, which is promptly brought and placed before him.

The stewardess asked the preacher if he wanted a drink?

Appalled by the suggestion, the Preacher replied, "I'd rather be tied up and taken advantage of by women of ill-repute, then let liquor touch my lips.

The cowboy then hands the drink back to the stewardess and says, "Me too, I did not know we had a choice."

Who are Jesus's favorite gospel singers?

Mary Mary.

Why weren't Moses and Jesus allowed to volunteer at the Red Cross and United Way?

They are non-prophet organizations.

Did you know Moses and Joshua had a huge argument?

They parted ways.

Who was the youngest person in the Bible to use curse words?

Job, he cursed the day he was born.

What type of insurance did Noah have on the Arc?

Flood insurance.

What was Jezebel's and Humpty Dumpty's favorite month?

**October!
They both
had big falls.**

What did the all the people sitting around the fat lady, who farted loudly in church say?

Pew.

What does a accountant, scientist, and rabbit all have in common?

Numbers is their favorite book of the Bible.

One night, Jesus and the disciples were hanging out at a bar.

Jesus asks the bartender for a pitcher of water. This was so he could turn water into wine.

One of the disciples asked," Jesus, why can't you buy a round like everybody else?

Jokingly, Jesus replied "Jesus saves."

What is did Lot say to his wife before exiting Sodom?

Lighten up.

What is Satan's favorite food?

Deviled eggs.

Did you know there is a rumor that Jesus was a beautiful woman?

That is why 12 men followed her around.

What do you say to God after he sneezes?

I don't know. I never heard God sneeze.

Did you know there is evidence that Satan is a cross-dresser?

The Devil wears Prada, The Devil in a blue dress and known as She-Devil.

What do religion and sports have in common?

The emotions, the passion and the crazy fanatics that give each a bad name.

What happened when the Widow sold Olive Oil to patrons.

Popeye the Sailor was angry.

Peter, Paul and Mary walked into a bar.

The bartender says, "I love your music."

What is God's favorite pick up line?

"What are you doing here? I did not know you left heaven?"

At the Last Supper, Jesus breaks the bread, and says"this is my body."
And then, he pours the wine and says " this is my blood."he Last Supper, Jesus breaks the bread, "this is my body."
Suprisingly Jesus rips a loud fart.
Jesus smiles at the men, and says "That was the fish."

Have you heard the rumors about Christianity going around?

Nevermind, I shouldn't spread it.

Did you know Jezebel had a drug addicition?

She was a cracked head.

What was Lot Wife's like after leaving Sodom?

Very Salty.

What do sidewalks, toliet paper and Jezebel have in common?

They all deal with cracks.

How did Delilah get into Samson's secure house?

She picked his locks.

What name did the people buying & selling at the temple call Jesus, after he flipped the tables?

A flipping prophet

Michael Jordan and Jesus walk into a bar.

The exicted bartender goes "Oh my goodness I can't believe you are here."

He continued"You are the greatest. The things you have done. The miracles you did. I have always been a follower and fan.

At that time, Michael Jordan says "Thanks. Would you like an autograph?"

"No. Who are you?" askes the bartender, "I was talking about Jesus Christ."

What do you call a religious quaterback?

A Passtor.

What do the Woman with issue of blood and Hip Hop rappers have in common?

They have mean flows.

Who did the
Pharoah of
Egypt talk to
when he was
sad or lonely?

His Mummy.

Where does The Potter's House do all its banking?

TD Banks.

What did the Pastor say when he was fishing and a fish jumped in the boat?

Holy Mackeral

Did you know Moses was well advanced in technology?

All the data received came from a cloud.

What happened when Jesus farted?

Don't know. It took three days to smell.

A Preacher tells his congregation, next Sunday, I plan to preach about the sin of lying. Please read Ruth 5, for next Sunday.

The next Sunday, the Preacher asks if the all read Ruth 5, every hand raises.

The Preacher smiled and says Ruth only has 4 chapters. I will now proceed with my sermon on the sin of lying

How is your family's Thanksgiving Holiday similiar to the apple situation of Adam & Eve in the Garden of Eden?

Doesn't your family argue about the meal. Then, isn't somebody is kicked out of the house.

Jesus and the Vampire are at Moses' yearly barbeque.

But, the two never have the steak.

What did Jesus do to the Disciples as he walked on the stormy ocean?

He waved.

Made in United States
Troutdale, OR
09/21/2024

23011856R00046